LOVE WITH ALL YOUR HEART

NAVIGATING FAMILY, FRIENDSHIPS, AND DATING

PRESENTED TO

BY

DATE

Lifeway Press®
Brentwood, Tennessee

© 2023 Lifeway Press®
Reprinted Dec. 2024

No part of this work may be reproduced or transmitted in any form or by any means, electronic or mechanical, including photocopying and recording, or by any information storage or retrieval system, except as may be expressly permitted in writing by the publisher. Requests for permission should be addressed in writing to Lifeway Press®, 200 Powell Place, Suite 100, Brentwood, TN, 37027

ISBN 978-1-0877-8479-3
Item 005842351
Dewey Decimal Classification Number: 242
Subject Heading: DEVOTIONAL LITERATURE / BIBLE STUDY AND TEACHING / GOD

Printed in the United States of America.

Student Ministry Publishing
Lifeway Resources
200 Powell Place, Suite 100
Brentwood, Tennessee 37027

We believe that the Bible has God for its author; salvation for its end; truth, without any mixture of error, for its matter; and that all Scripture is totally true and trustworthy. To review Lifeway's doctrinal guideline, please visit www.lifeway.com/doctrinalguideline.

Unless otherwise noted, all Scripture quotations are taken from the Christian Standard Bible®, Copyright © 2017 by Holman Bible Publishers. Used by permission. Christian Standard Bible® and CSB® are federally registered trademarks of Holman Bible Publishers.

publishing team

Director, Student Ministry
Ben Trueblood

Manager, Student Ministry Publishing
Karen Daniel

Writer
Stephanie Cross

Content Editor
Kyle Wiltshire

Production Editor
April-Lyn Caouette

Graphic Designer
Shiloh Stufflebeam
Grace Morgan

TABLE OF CONTENTS

04
INTRO

05
GETTING STARTED

06
FAMILY

40
FRIENDS

74
DATING

108
TOXIC TRAITS

110
TOXIC LOVE

INTRO

Our culture is obsessed with finding "true love." Is it possible that the idea doesn't quite mean what we think it means? Maybe the "fairy tale" kind of true love falls flat because ultimately it doesn't satisfy our deepest longings to be known and loved.

We were born longing for love deep in our souls. Not the cheap kind that comes on chalky candy hearts but a love that is beyond our understanding (see Isa. 55:8-9). God, the Author of life, is also the Author of love. Who better to write the story of love than the One who *is* love?

Love is so complex that the ancient Greeks used eight different words to describe it. Four of the most common are *agape*, *eros*, *phileo*, and *storge*. *Agape* is unconditional love, the kind that God has for us. *Eros* is romantic or sexual love. *Phileo* is the affectionate love we have for friends or family ("brotherly love"). *Storge* describes love for family.[1]

Unconditional love is a part of God's character. It's bigger than what we feel in our hearts or what's going on in the world. It doesn't rest on anything other than who God is. This love is a gift to us from God, seen most clearly in Him sending His Son to die for our sins and offer us eternal life.

Out of the love He gives, we are called to give love to others. That's where the other types of love come in. God calls us to love our family, friends, and significant others well. Over the next thirty days we will break it all down and discover how to love our families, friends, and the people we date out of the great love that God has for us.

---

1. Spiros Zodhiates, *The Complete Word Study Dictionary: New Testament*, s.v. "philostorgos" (Chattanooga, TN: AMG Publishers, 2000); David Lanier, "Love," in *Holman Illustrated Bible Dictionary*, edited by Chad Brand et al. (Nashville, TN: Holman Bible Publishers, 2003), 1054.

GETTING STARTED

This devotional contains thirty days of content, broken down into sections. Each day is divided into three elements—**discover**, **delight**, and **display**—to help you grow in your faith and guide your time in God's Word.

DISCOVER

This section helps you examine the passage in light of who God is and determine what it says about your identity in relationship to Him. Included here is the daily Scripture reading and key verses, along with illustrations and commentary to guide you as you learn more about God's Word.

DELIGHT

In this section, you'll be challenged by questions and activities that help you see how God is alive and active in every detail of His Word and your life.

DISPLAY

Here's where you take action. This section calls you to apply what you've learned through each day.

> Each day also includes a prayer activity at the conclusion of the devotion.

Throughout the devotional, you'll also find extra items to help you connect with the topic personally, such as Scripture memory verses and interactive articles.

SECTION 1

FAMILY

Family can be complicated. No family is perfect, and we can see that clearly throughout Scripture. But we also see God's design for family to be a foundation of love and learning before we're sent out into the world. God's love for us steers us through the squabbles, laughter, and love of family.

DAY 1

FOR THE WIN

READ MARK 12:28-34.

Jesus answered, "The most important is: Listen, Israel! The Lord our God, the Lord is one. Love the Lord your God with all your heart, with all your soul, with all your mind, and with all your strength."
— Mark 12:29-30

DISCOVER

When we love something, we put everything we have into it. In sports, an exhausted athlete might say, "I left it all on the field." A wiped-out singer might say after a solo performance that she "left it all on the stage." This doesn't mean they came away from these experiences empty; rather, they're the best kind of exhausted because they made every effort as they gave their best to go for the win.

In this passage, the scribe—a religious scholar—asked Jesus for a game plan of sorts. He wanted to know: *What's the most important command for me to obey?* In other words, *What's the most important thing for me to know about following God?* Jesus gave the scribe the perfect winning strategy, one that's clear but isn't easy to follow: *Love God with all that you are.*

It's not just about showing love with our actions or speaking love with our words. Going for the win in following God means loving Him first and most, then loving others with the same love He gives to us. Tomorrow we'll look more at loving others. That's also when we'll start to see how loving God the most is the key to loving our family and others well.

DELIGHT

What does it looks like to love God with all your heart, all your soul, all your mind, and all your strength?

The scribe said rightly that "there is no one else except [God]" (v. 32). When is it difficult to love God most?

DISPLAY

Being "all in" with God means knowing we're His, loving Him most, and giving every effort to serve Him with all that we are. All people are created in the image of God, and all of us have different God-given talents that we can use to glorify Him. Think about how God has gifted you and write out one way you can use those gifts to show God that you love Him.

Love starts with God, since He Himself *is* love. Ask God to help you love Him well, to love yourself as He loves you, and to love others the same way. Pray that God would help you see ways to show love to Him and others this week.

DAY 2

LOVE FROM GOD

READ MARK 12:28-34 AGAIN.

"The second is, Love your neighbor as yourself. There is no other command greater than these."
— Mark 12:31

DISCOVER

After Jesus explained that the most important command is to love God with all that we are, He said the next most important command is to "love your neighbor as yourself." In Luke's version of this same story, the scribe asked, "Who is my neighbor?" (Luke 10:29). Like many of us, it seems that the scribe wanted to know just how far to extend this love.

In response, Jesus told a story about a Samaritan who cared for a wounded man after a priest and a Levite had both gone out of their way to avoid him. Jews in Jesus's day looked down on Samaritans, so this was a big deal. The men in Jesus's story—all from different backgrounds and places in life—had walked the same road and had seen the same wounded man. Only one stopped—a hated Samaritan! And he went all in! He bandaged the man's wounds, took him to an inn, and paid for his stay and care.

Simply put: Jesus said we are called to love whomever God puts in our path with a love that comes straight from God. When we love God the most, He empowers us to love others, no matter who they are. And often the easiest people for us to take for granted are the members of our families. So, loving others as we love ourselves begins at home with our family members.

DELIGHT

What does it look like to love your neighbor as yourself? When is it tough to do this?

Read Acts 1:8 and Galatians 5:22-23. How does God empower us to love His way? Why is it important for us to remember this?

DISPLAY

Sometimes the people we struggle to love most are the people closest to us. Think about the people in your family, or those you consider your family, and write out each name below. What were your most recent interactions with those people like? Were you happy, excited, frustrated, upset? Beside each name, write out "God calls me to love _____ (name) no matter what." Flip back to this page as a reminder any time you're struggling to love someone close to you.

Ask God to show you the people He has placed on your path to love. Pray that He would help you see how each specific person needs to be loved. Ask Him for the grace to love when things get tough and a heart that desires to keep growing in love.

DAY 3

HOW TO HONOR

READ EPHESIANS 6:1-3.

Children, obey your parents in the Lord, because this is right.
— Ephesians 6:1

DISCOVER

God designed families for our good and His glory. He designed parents to love and care for their children and teach them to follow Him. The call to "obey your parents" means to listen to their commands and guidance. The instruction to "honor your parents" means to respect them with your words, actions, and even your thoughts.

In healthy family situations, obeying and honoring our parents brings good and joy into our lives, even if it might not seem fun in the moment (see v. 3). Godly parents can be a great resource for sound advice, correction, community, and prayer.

It's important to know that when sin broke into the world through Adam and Eve, that sin seeped into every area of human life, including family. And sometimes this leads to a world of hurt. But God's commands are intended to be for our good and His glory. Obeying your parents should never mean doing something that is harmful to you or someone else in any way, nor should it ever mean doing something that goes against God's Word. If this is your experience, know that this is not God's design or His desire for you, and it breaks His heart. This is why our first call is to love God, then to love others. We obey Him above all.

DELIGHT

Why did Paul say children should obey their parents (v. 2)? What reason did he add in verse 3?

When do you struggle to obey your parents? How can you honor them even when it's hard to obey?

What's difficult about honoring your parents? How do these verses encourage you to honor your parents even when it's difficult?

DISPLAY

Obeying your parents may seem like a pretty simple concept: just do what they ask you to do. But the idea of honoring them might be a bit more difficult to grasp because honoring is more about the attitude behind your actions. For some of us, this might mean respecting and loving someone as a person made in the image of God but not obeying instructions they give us that are harmful to us and others—in other words, instructions that don't come from God. Think about your situation, and ask yourself: What's typically in my heart when my parents ask me to do something or want to spend time with me? (Tip: your physical responses—the feelings you have in your body—are a good indicator of what's in your heart.) As you think about the answer to this question, reflect on how you can go beyond simple obedience to truly honor your parents.

Pray for your parents or guardians. If you're in a great situation, thank God for that. If your family situation is difficult, talk to God about that too. Ask Him to help you honor your parents even if you can't always obey. Pray that God would help you know the difference.

DAY 4

GROWING WITH JESUS

READ LUKE 2:41-52.

Then he went down with them and came to Nazareth and was obedient to them. His mother kept all these things in her heart. And Jesus increased in wisdom and stature, and in favor with God and with people.
— Luke 2:51-52

DISCOVER

Have you ever thought back on what your world was like when you were a little kid? How things that scared you then seem silly now? How activities that used to entertain you seem boring now? How big your pretend world would get, no matter where you were?

Every one of us has a history of days, weeks, months, and years that lead up to where we are today. But we don't know much about what Jesus was like as a kid; most of the Gospels focus on the three years of His ministry, death, and resurrection. Luke is the only Gospel writer to include any details at all about Jesus's childhood. He kindly gives us a glimpse into the life of twelve-year-old Jesus, and the story teaches us a few things about how we can live God-honoring lives, no matter our age.

Jesus obeyed His parents. When they found Him after anxiously searching for three days, He went home with them. Jesus also obeyed God. He had spent those three days learning and asking questions of the leaders in the temple. As Jesus obeyed His parents and God, He grew in every way and gained favor from people and His heavenly Father. When we honor our parents and honor God, we will grow in these same ways.

DELIGHT

What did Jesus do in this passage to increase in wisdom? How can you follow His example?

What did Jesus do to increase in favor with God and people? How can you follow His example?

DISPLAY

Did your parents, grandparents, or guardians keep track of your height by marking it on a wall or door frame? Have you ever looked at baby clothes and wondered how you were ever that tiny? Does it ever surprise you when you think about what grade you're in now or how close you are to graduation? We mark our growth in all kinds of ways, but it can be difficult to mark our spiritual growth—particularly the way we're growing in love (see 1 Thess. 3:12). If you want to know if you're growing spiritually and in love, ask yourself: *Am I closer to God today than I was yesterday? How can I grow closer to God tomorrow than I am today? How am I loving others better than I was last year? How can I grow in loving those around me even more, including my family?* Journal your responses in the space below. Use a separate notebook or piece of paper if you need more space.

Thank God for giving us Jesus as our ultimate example for how to live for Him. Pray that He would help you see the ways you can grow in your relationship with Him, and praise Him for the ways He has already helped you grow.

DAY 5

GOD COMES FIRST

READ JOHN 2:1-12.

"Fill the jars with water," Jesus told them. So they filled them to the brim. Then he said to them, "Now draw some out and take it to the headwaiter." And they did.
— John 2:7-8

DISCOVER

Imagine what it would be like if you got to celebrate your birthday for an entire week or even two weeks. Who would you invite? Where would you go? What would you do? This might be a little tough to imagine since it isn't the norm for most of us, but in Jesus's day, celebrations like weddings lasted for a week.

During that week, it would have been a huge embarrassment for the bride and groom to run out of any supplies, like food and beverages. Unfortunately for the bride and groom at a wedding Jesus attended, they ran out of wine. Jesus's mother, Mary, was involved in the festivities and noticed the problem—and she knew exactly who could solve it: her son, who is God in flesh!

Despite how it might seem, Jesus's responses to His mother weren't disrespectful. Jesus addressed her as "woman"—a term of respect in His day—just before reminding her that He would ultimately obey His Father. Even though it wasn't yet time for Jesus to reveal Himself as the Messiah, He was able to honor His mother's request while remaining obedient to His Father and glorifying Him with this miracle. Jesus commanded, the servants obeyed, and the water became wine. In the book of John, this was the first miracle Jesus ever performed.

DELIGHT

What do Mary's words in verse 5 tell you about her trust in and relationship with Jesus?

How did Jesus honor God in this passage? How did Jesus also honor His mother, even though obedience to God was His priority?

Why is it important for us to know that obedience to God comes first and to honor our parents when we obey God?

DISPLAY

Jesus said, "If you love me, you will keep my commands" (John 14:15). God doesn't ask us to give love without first giving it Himself. He has offered us the gift of His great love through Jesus, and believers respond to His love by loving and obeying God in return. God is a perfect Father, and His commands are perfect and for our good. Our parents won't always be perfect, but we can show them love by being obedient to their godly commands and requests. Write out a few godly commands or requests your parents have made, then write out how you can obey in a way that shows love and brings honor.

Ask God to help you see where He's leading you and what He wants you to do. Pray that as you obey Him, He will give you the desire and heart to obey the godly commands that your parents or guardians give you.

DAY 6

COMMITTED TO COMPASSION

READ JOHN 19:25-27.

When Jesus saw his mother and the disciple he loved standing there, he said to his mother, "Woman, here is your son."
— John 19:26

DISCOVER

Who are your favorite people—those you spend the most time with or the people who make you feel included and loved? Maybe these people are in your family, but maybe they're friends or mentors who have become like family to you.

In today's verses, we see two of the people closest to Jesus. The scene takes place right in the middle of Jesus's crucifixion, with several of His followers looking on. But Jesus's eyes rested on John (the "Beloved Disciple" and author of the Gospel of John) and Mary (Jesus's mother). Despite the pain He must have been experiencing, Jesus turned His heart toward caring for His mother.

It seems that at this point, Joseph (Mary's husband) had died, and none of Jesus's half-brothers believed in Him yet. So Jesus instructed John to take care of His mother after His death. Not only was Jesus honoring His mother as Scripture commanded and obeying His heavenly Father perfectly, He was also making sure His mother would be provided for. It's only a few verses later that we see Jesus taking His final breath (see v. 30). But the last verse in this section of Scripture assures us that Mary would be cared for as Jesus hoped and commanded: "And from that hour the disciple took her into his home" (v. 27).

DELIGHT

Why does it matter that Jesus took care of His mother even as He was being crucified?

Think about the timing of Jesus's placing Mary into John's care: He essentially instructed John to care for her like he would care for his own mother. What does this tell you about Jesus's focus and heart for people?

DISPLAY

While you might not be called to provide care for your parents or others by taking them into your home, you can look at Jesus's example to see how to love and honor those who care for you, even when you're stressed out. Examine Jesus's attitude compared with what was going on around Him. He had just taken on the world's sin (past, present, and future) and was dying on a cross, but He still showed compassion and love for His mother. Think about how you respond to people when you're stressed and journal how you want to tweak those responses (or create new ones) based on Jesus's example.

Ask God to show you how to honor those in authority over you, even on the tough days. Pray that He would show you how to care for others well, no matter what's going on in your life.

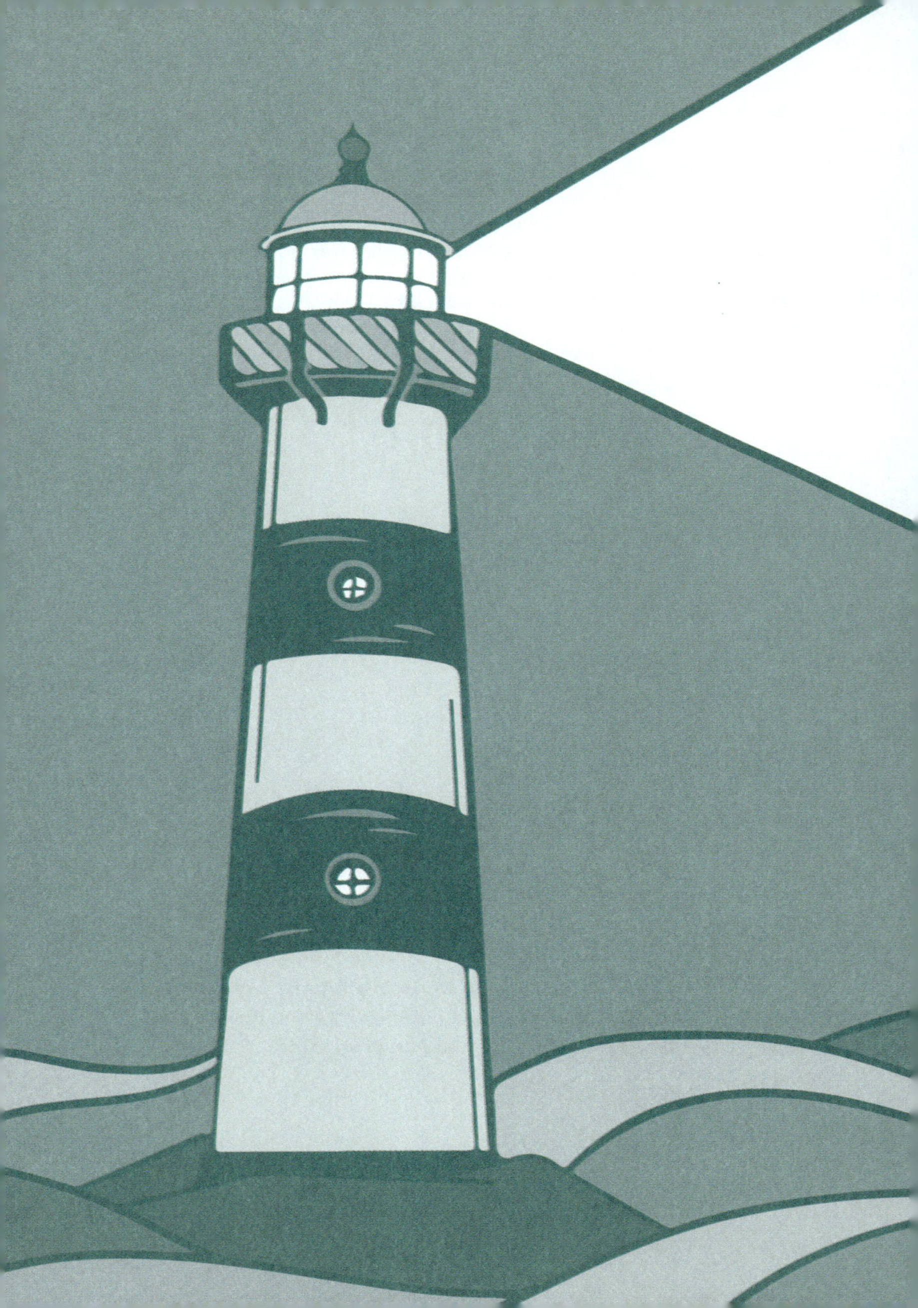

MARK 12:29-31

Jesus answered, "The most important is Listen, Israel! The Lord our God, the Lord is one. Love the Lord your God with all your heart, with all your soul, with all your mind, and with all your strength. The second is, Love your neighbor as yourself. There is no other command greater than these."

MEMORY VERSE

DAY 7

LOVE IN LISTENING

READ PROVERBS 1:8-19.

Listen, my son, to your father's instruction, and don't reject your mother's teaching, for they will be a garland of favor on your head and pendants around your neck.
— Proverbs 1:8-9

DISCOVER

Have you ever tried to have a serious conversation with someone who is distractedly scrolling and tapping away on a screen? How do you feel when people cut you off to tell you a related story—about themselves? Neither of these attitudes make us feel like our words are important.

Listening well is vital to loving well—and listening is more than hearing. Listening is about focusing on what others say; it's not about filling pauses or rushing to the next thing. Listening is intentional.

The word "listen" in this passage carries the idea of undivided attention and quick obedience, with undertones of respect, love, care, and contentedness.[2] When our parents give instructions, this is not always how we want to respond, right? Sometimes listening and obeying seems like a chore. We may want to roll our eyes, talk back, or ignore the person altogether. But Scripture teaches us to do the opposite: listen, and be content and respectful as we do.

When godly parents set boundaries or give rules, warnings, and corrections, it's to make sure their kids are living the full and abundant life God promises (see John 10:10). When we obey the God-honoring instruction of our parents, it leads us to honor our parents and God.

---

2. Blue Letter Bible, s.v. "H8085 - Sama - Strong's Hebrew Lexicon (KJV)," accessed February 2, 2023, https://www.blueletterbible.org/lexicon/h8085/kjv/wlc/0-1/.

DELIGHT

When can it be tough to listen to your parents with undivided attention and quick obedience?

How does listening to godly instruction help us? How does it show love to others, including God?

What are some rewards you've experienced from listening to godly instruction? What are some consequences you've faced for ignoring it?

DISPLAY

We all get distracted sometimes. Take a minute to examine your attitude about listening by answering the following questions.

How often would you say you listen with undivided attention?

| 0 | 1 | 2 | 3 | 4 | 5 |

Never   **Sometimes**   **Always!**

How often do you do what you're asked right when you're asked to do it?

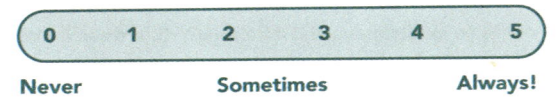

| 0 | 1 | 2 | 3 | 4 | 5 |

Never   **Sometimes**   **Always!**

How often do your attitude, tone of voice, body language, and actions communicate respect, love, care, and contentedness?

| 0 | 1 | 2 | 3 | 4 | 5 |

Never   **Sometimes**   **Always!**

Jot down a sentence of prayer or a goal for how you want to improve in these areas.

> Pray that God would help you see where you aren't listening well and how you can tune your heart to listen better out of love for Him and others. Ask Him to help you want to listen and obey, and ask for His help to lean into the Holy Spirit's leading in your life.

DAY 8

THE MUDDY MIDDLE

READ GENESIS 4:1-16.

Then the Lord said to Cain, "Why are you furious? And why do you look despondent? If you do what is right, won't you be accepted? But if you do not do what is right, sin is crouching at the door. Its desire is for you, but you must rule over it."
— Genesis 4:6-7

DISCOVER

We usually know when we're doing something wrong, and we often try to hide it rather than admit it. We probably also wouldn't admit the uneasy feeling deep inside when we're close with someone who's doing the right thing when we're not. Cain, Adam and Eve's firstborn son, was stuck in the middle of these two feelings.

Cain took some of his harvest to God as an offering (see v. 3), but his brother Abel gave "some of the firstborn of his flock" (v. 4). This may seem insignificant, but God asked for the first and best. Only "some" wouldn't cut it. This is why Abel's sacrifice pleased God but Cain's didn't. Abel's was from his best; Cain's was more of an afterthought.

The Bible says that "Cain was furious" and more than a little down (see v. 5). It's so easy to let feelings of bitterness and jealousy creep in when we feel like someone else is doing it better—especially with family. But Cain let those feelings go unchecked, and they escalated to the point of murder.

Even in the muddy middle of our own feelings and jealousies and mistakes, we are called to pursue God above all else. When we are filled with His love, sin isn't in charge—God is.

DELIGHT

God warned Cain about what would happen if he didn't do the right thing (see v. 6). How has God warned us about sin? What's a warning that stands out to you?

What did God say would happen if Cain did what was right (see v. 6)? What do you think that means?

Why is it easy to respond with sarcasm or a bad attitude like Cain did in verse 9?

DISPLAY

Let's take a quick look at the ways Cain responded to this whole situation: (1) He was angry and down. (2) He ignored God's warning. (3) He gave in to sin. (4) He responded to God with a bad attitude. (5) He was unrepentant.

Think about a situation you're struggling with. Now, let's flip these five responses and look at better ways to respond. Jot notes in the space provided about how each response applies to your situation.

1 — **Recognize the wrong.**

2 — **Be open to God's warnings in His Word and through the Holy Spirit.**

3 — **Run from sinning further (see 2 Tim. 2:22; James 4:7).**

4 — **Respond to conviction.**

5 — **Repent of sin.**

Pray that God would help you see any anger you hold in your heart for those around you, including your siblings. Ask God to forgive you and help you see how to respond to that person and situation.

DAY 9

TO SIT OR TO SERVE?

READ LUKE 10:38-42.

The Lord answered her, "Martha, Martha, you are worried and upset about many things, but one thing is necessary. Mary has made the right choice, and it will not be taken away from her."
— Luke 10:41-42

DISCOVER

Have you ever been doing exactly what you were supposed to do while a sibling or classmate seemed to just be taking his or her time or ignoring the instruction? It can be super frustrating when we feel like we're working hard and doing the right things while others aren't. But what about the times when the right thing is less obvious? Two sisters, Mary and Martha, found themselves in this kind of situation in today's verses.

Jesus came to visit the sisters in their home. Martha hurried around, acting as the perfect hostess. But Mary simply sat down with Jesus. Martha was so frustrated with her sister that she even tried to get Jesus on her side—but Jesus didn't respond the way Martha expected Him to. Can you imagine Martha's shock? Mary's choice—sitting instead of serving—was best?

When it comes to what's best, our perspective has to shift: worshiping Jesus and loving others as He loves should always come first. The task we need to get done may not happen immediately, but keeping Jesus first in our hearts helps us grow healthier relationships with our siblings and family.

DELIGHT

Do Jesus's words to Martha surprise you? Why or why not?

How does your attitude sometimes reflect Martha's? What do you need to shift to have an attitude that's consistently more like Mary's?

DISPLAY

Martha's desire to serve wasn't wrong—it just wasn't the best choice in the moment. Her working distracted her from loving her sister and worshiping Jesus. While there are things we have to get done, sometimes our "have to" list keeps us from loving others well and worshiping Jesus. Think about your life over the last week. Has it shown that Jesus is first in your heart? Consider a specific example and rewrite the ending, showing how you could have kept Jesus as your focus and how that might have affected your interactions with your family.

Pray that God would help you see how to keep Jesus first and to recognize the right response when your daily life is interrupted. Ask God to help you worship Him above all and love your siblings and family well.

DAY 10

EVEN NOW

READ JOHN 1:1-44.

Now a man was sick—Lazarus from Bethany, the village of Mary and her sister Martha. Mary was the one who anointed the Lord with perfume and wiped his feet with her hair, and it was her brother Lazarus who was sick. So the sisters sent a message to him: "Lord, the one you love is sick."
— John 11:1-3

DISCOVER

Mary and Martha—the sisters from yesterday's devotion—needed to get in touch with Jesus. Their brother was really sick and they loved him deeply. So they sent word to Jesus asking for help, saying, "Lord, the one you love is sick" (v. 3).

Jesus didn't come immediately. Instead, He delayed. When Jesus arrived in Bethany, both sisters acknowledged that their brother wouldn't have died if Jesus had been there (see vv. 21,32), but Martha pointed out something important: "Yet even now I know that whatever you ask from God, God will give you" (v. 22). And it was true: Jesus would raise Lazarus from the dead.

But the most important thing Jesus said was: "I am the resurrection and the life, the one who believes in me, even if he dies, will live. Everyone who believes in me will never die" (vv. 25-26). When the sisters requested Jesus's help for healing in the physical realm, they didn't understand the extent of Jesus's ability to give new life. But we have the rest of the story, and we know Jesus can give new, eternal life to those who were once spiritually dead (see John 3:16; Rom. 6:4; 2 Cor. 5:17).

These sisters called upon the Lord for their brother. Are you calling upon the Lord for the spiritual health of your sisters and brothers?

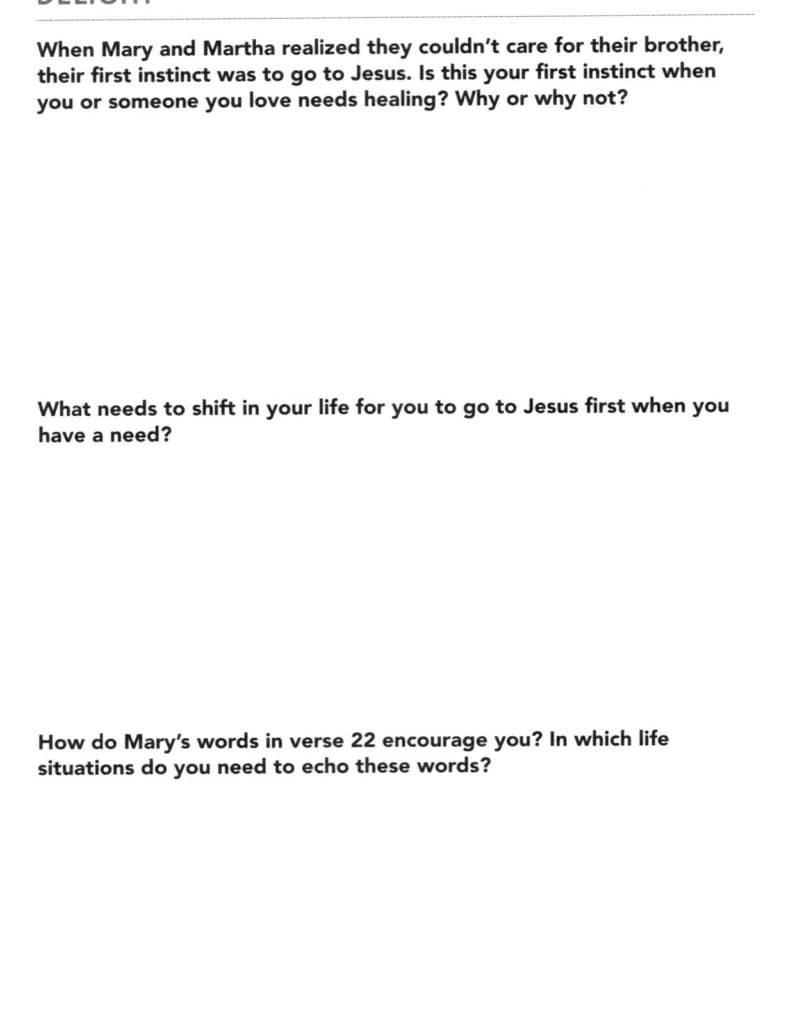

DELIGHT

When Mary and Martha realized they couldn't care for their brother, their first instinct was to go to Jesus. Is this your first instinct when you or someone you love needs healing? Why or why not?

What needs to shift in your life for you to go to Jesus first when you have a need?

How do Mary's words in verse 22 encourage you? In which life situations do you need to echo these words?

DISPLAY

When we seek help for the people we love, we tend to go to other people who love them because we know they have our loved ones' best interests at heart too. Jesus's capacity for love is beyond our understanding. Who could love us more than the One who *is* love? No matter whether our sickness is physical, mental, emotional, or spiritual, Jesus is always the ultimate Healer (though sometimes His care can come through professionals with the skills to help us, too!). Answer each question below by writing in names of people who fit the description. Pray for those people every day this week.

Who in your family needs physical healing?

Who in your family is struggling with their mental health?

Who in your family is going through a painful emotional experience?

Who in your family is struggling in their faith?

Ask God to help you run to Him first when those you love are hurting. Pray that He would help you see how you can influence your family and loved ones for Him.

SECTION 2

FRIENDS

Some of our most important relationships are the ones we have with our friends. We all need people who are seeking God from a similar place in life to walk alongside us, encourage us, and call us out—in love—when we need it. In this section, we'll look at what it means to find and build friendships centered on godly love, and we'll see what it really means to love our friends well.

DAY 11

SACRIFICE

READ JOHN 15:9-17.

"No one has greater love than this: to lay down his life for his friends."
— John 15:13

DISCOVER

What do you think of when you hear the word "sacrifice"? In a biblical context, maybe you think of animal sacrifice in the Old Testament or Jesus dying on the cross. In our modern everyday context, you might think of a person serving in the military or a single mom who works three jobs to provide for her kids.

But let's put a more concrete meaning behind the word. According to the Merriam-Webster Dictionary, sacrifice is "an act of offering to [God] something precious; surrender of something for the sake of something else; to suffer loss of, give up . . . especially for an ideal, belief, or end."[3]

When it comes down to it, our ultimate definition of sacrifice is Jesus. He showed us God's absolute and unconditional love when He died on the cross to offer salvation to all people. Once we trust in Him to save us from our sin, we receive the Holy Spirit, who helps us love Jesus and love others. This includes learning to live sacrificially for our friends.

Most likely, you won't literally need to die for your friends. This passage's application for us is more about the heart behind the action. Simply put, we should be willing to give up what is most precious to us for the good of our friends and the glory of God.

---

3. Merriam-Webster Dictionary Online, s.v. "sacrifice," accessed February 8, 2023, https://www.merriam-webster.com/dictionary/sacrifice.

DELIGHT

Highlight or circle the word that appears most often in verses 9-10. How did Jesus use this word to help His disciples?

How does Jesus's command in verse 12 connect to His statement in verse 13?

Who are Jesus's friends? How does this change your understanding of verse 13?

DISPLAY

Write the names of your closest friends in the space provided below. Then, consider two things about them: (1) What are their greatest struggles? and (2) What are their deepest needs? Jot down a word or two by each name to answer those questions. Now, read Matthew 25:31-40, 1 Corinthians 10:23-31, Hebrews 13:16, and James 2:14-17. Ask yourself: *What could God be calling me to give up so that I can support my friends in their struggles? What is God calling me to give up so that I can meet my friends' deepest needs?* Use the remaining space to write your response.

Ask God to help you really see your friends and to be open to whatever you need to "lay down" to love them well. Pray that God would give you the strength and desire to love others this way.

DAY 12

I'LL BE THERE FOR YOU

READ PROVERBS 17:17.

A friend loves at all times, and a brother is born for a difficult time.
— Proverbs 17:17

DISCOVER

Have you ever thought about the way we use the word "all"? Maybe we say someone does something "all the time," or that we have done "all we can," or that "all people" say or do something. But in those situations, how often do we truly mean always, in everything, or everyone?

In Hebrew, the word "all" in this verse carries a sense of wholeness, completeness, and totality.[4] To love our friends this way means that instead of being jealous when good things happen to them, we love them. Instead of ghosting them when they're going through a tough time, we love them. A whole, complete, and total love is the kind of love that God gives us. It's the kind of love that stays and says, "I'll be there for you, no matter what, in every way I can."

That sounds pretty good, right? We certainly want this kind of love for ourselves too. While we don't give to get, we attract our friends by the type of friend we are. Simply put: be the kind of friend you want to have. This might seem tough or even impossible on some days, but when it does, remember that God was this kind of friend to you first. He is the best friend we could ever have, and through His Word and His Holy Spirit, He teaches us how to be that kind of friend to others.

---

4. Blue Letter Bible, s.v. "H3605 - Kōl - Strong's Hebrew Lexicon (KJV)," accessed February 9, 2023, https://www.blueletterbible.org/lexicon/h3605/kjv/wlc/0-1/.

DELIGHT

When is it difficult to love others well?

Who loves you this way? How can you show these people you appreciate their love and friendship?

What needs to change in your life for you to be the kind of friend you want to have?

DISPLAY

Make a statement of commitment to love your best friends. First, think about your closest friends and write their names below. Beside each name, write your commitment in the format of: "I'll be there for you even if/when _____." Try to choose something specific to each person. Consider writing the commitments out on note cards and giving them to your friends. (If a friend is involved in something dangerous, don't put yourself in danger trying to help. Go to the appropriate authorities—like parents, teachers, pastors, or coaches—for help.)

Ask God to help you love your friends completely, totally, and wholly, just like He loves us. Pray that He would help you see when loving your friends means telling difficult truths and how to do that as well as how to encourage them on normal days.

DAY 13

RICH AND VIBRANT

READ ECCLESIASTES 4:9-12.

Two are better than one because they have a good reward for their efforts.
— Ecclesiastes 4:9

DISCOVER

The Hebrew word in Ecclesiastes translated as "futile", "vanity", or "meaningless" (depending on translation) is used frequently. Solomon labeled many things as "futile," like accomplishments, seeking pleasure, and riches. This word means emptiness, a breath, or a vapor.[5]

But out of all the things Solomon calls futile, friendship isn't one of them.[6] In fact, he points to friendship as being the opposite: it brings fullness of life; it's meaningful; it's strength; it's absolutely priceless.

In these verses, Solomon points out that friends can accomplish more together (see v. 9), help each other up when one falls (see v. 10), take care of each other (see v. 11), and protect each other (see v. 12). Then Solomon, the man God gifted with extraordinary wisdom, throws in one final thought: "A cord of three strands is not easily broken" (v. 12).

The point is this: community matters. God the Father—who Himself lives in community with the Son and the Holy Spirit—created us for relationship with Him and others (see Gen. 1:26). When we combine those two things, putting God at the center of our friendships, all of life becomes rich and vibrant, no matter how dark it may sometimes seem.

---

5. Blue Letter Bible, s.v. "H1892 - Hebel - Strong's Hebrew Lexicon (KJV)," accessed February 10, 2023, https://www.blueletterbible.org/lexicon/h1892/kjv/wlc/0-1/.
6. Duane A. Garrett, "Ecclesiastes," in *CSB Study Bible: Notes*, ed. Edwin A. Blum and Trevin Wax (Nashville, TN: Holman Bible Publishers, 2017), 1010.

DELIGHT

When are you tempted to believe that being alone is better than having community? How does this passage show you a better way?

Though the author doesn't specifically point to God as the "third strand," why is it important for us to have God at the center of every relationship?

How could God being the center of your friendships change the way you relate to others? To God?

DISPLAY

As a sort of "friendship check-up," let's give each of your friends (and then you!) a superlative as we go through Solomon's qualities of friendships.

First, write out the names of two to five of your closest friends.

Who is most likely to help you get more done?

Most Productive: %

Who is most likely to help you up when you fall—without laughing? What about when you make a mistake?

Most Helpful: %

Who is most likely to take care of you when you're cold, tired, hungry, or feeling sick?

Most Compassionate: %

Who is most likely to protect you or stand up for you if someone tries to harm you?

Most Protective: %

Now, go back through each one, and write a percentage indicating how likely you are to do the same for that friend.

Ask God to help you be the kind of friend who helps, serves, shows compassion, and protects. Thank God for good friends who do the same for you. Pray that you all would keep God at the center of your friendships.

DAY 14

FAITH AND FRIENDSHIP

READ PROVERBS 27:17.

Iron sharpens iron, and one person sharpens another.
— Proverbs 27:17

DISCOVER

You might not be familiar with the idea of sharpening iron with iron, so think of it this way: If you don't sharpen a pencil, the point gets dull and makes it difficult to write. When you sharpen your pencil, the blade in the sharpener removes layers of wood and graphite to give you the point you need to write clearly.

Godly friends can be the pencil sharpeners of our spiritual lives. If we just keep pushing through life without pausing to consider what God might be asking us to do, convict us of, or trying to teach us, our faith becomes dull. It's easier to say "yes" to things we know aren't pleasing to God and more difficult to see His call on our lives.

God wants us to have vibrant faith (see John 10:10). The Holy Spirit helps us, but God also gives us relationships in our daily lives that make us better followers of Jesus. Godly friends and vibrant faith are closely linked.

But it would get old fast if our friends were always correcting us, right? It's important to know that these sharpening friendships rest in Jesus, who calls us to love each other just as He has loved us (see John 13:34). So, when our godly friends call us out on our sin, we must trust that their hearts are tuned to seek God's best for us. And when we confront our friends, we must always ask ourselves if our hearts are tuned the same way.

DELIGHT

What image comes to mind when you hear the words "iron sharpens iron"? How does this help you understand the way godly friends "sharpen" you?

How have you seen godly friendships sharpen your faith? How have you seen the opposite—friendships that draw you away from Jesus?

How does love motivate your friendships? If it doesn't, what needs to change so love of God and others is at the center of every relationship you have?

DISPLAY

Take a minute to think about all of your friendships. Write out the names of the three to five friends you're closest to, leaving space between each name. Under each name, describe how that person is sharpening your faith. If the person isn't sharpening your faith, write out one way you can sharpen his or her faith.

When you finish, spend some time praying over conversations you want to have with these friends, whether it's "thanks for calling me out" or "I need to talk to you about something." Trust that God will guide you in what's best, knowing He loves your friends more than you ever could.

Thank God for sending you godly friends to help you as you follow Him. If you don't have many godly friends, pray that God would bring those friends into your life or show you who they are if they're already there. Ask God to give you the courage to be a godly friend who sharpens others too.

DAY 15

TOXIC

READ PROVERBS 16:27-29.

A contrary person spreads conflict, and a gossip separates close friends.
— Proverbs 16:28

DISCOVER

Solomon let us in on a key truth: God made us for community, and when that community is filled with believers who sharpen each other out of love, faith grows. When we leave out love, the opposite happens. Today, we might use the word "toxic" to describe these relationships or the negative traits of people who aren't good for us.

Here's how Solomon described them. **Worthless** people (sometimes the this is translated "scoundrels" instead) rebel against godly authority and ideas. In this case, "worthless" doesn't mean that they have no value, but that they go looking to get into trouble and aren't kind with their words. **Contrary** people oppose others or desire to create conflict; they lie and they twist the truth others speak. **Gossips** complain and talk about others behind their backs but refuse to confront in truth and love. **Violent** types usually operate out of hearts filled with greed or hate. They will use others for their own gain and entice their friends to join them.[7]

Maybe you have some friends you might consider toxic or who have some toxic tendencies like the ones Solomon mentioned. The pattern of our lives follows the patterns of the people around us. So ask yourself: *Are my friends the kind who will build up or tear down?* Then, turn the question on yourself: *What kind of friend am I?*

---

7. David K. Stabnow, "Proverbs," in *CSB Study Bible: Notes*, ed. Edwin A. Blum and Trevin Wax (Nashville, TN: Holman Bible Publishers, 2017), 961.

DELIGHT

How would you summarize the four types of people Solomon mentioned?

Which of the characteristics have you seen in your own life? What are the characteristics you'd like to replace them with instead? How can you do that?

DISPLAY

All relationships that don't run on love will ultimately run out. Spend some time in prayer before answering the questions below. You can write your responses in a separate journal if you need more space:

Are there any toxic relationships in your life? If so, which ones?

What can you do about these relationships now?

Is there a relationship where you might be the one bringing in toxic traits? If so, how?

How can the four descriptions in today's verses help you build better relationships and friendships in the future?

Ask God to help you build strong and healthy friendships that seek to build up rather than tear down. Pray that God will make you into this kind of friend to others.

DAY 16

REPORTED

READ ROMANS 1:8-15.

For I want very much to see you, so that I may impart to you some spiritual gift to strengthen you, that is, to be mutually encouraged by each other's faith, both yours and mine.
— Romans 1:11-12

DISCOVER

Paul traveled through many regions sharing the gospel. He met a lot of believers, made a lot of friends, and visited many churches. While Paul had not yet been able to visit the church in Rome—despite desperately wanting to do so—he had heard about their faith because it was "being reported in all the world" (v. 8). Living in the center of pagan culture couldn't have been easy for the Roman believers, but they were thriving.

The believers in Rome weren't known for wrong behavior or misunderstandings in the faith. At the same time, they also weren't famous for their talented musicians, their pastor's fantastic sermons, or the size of their church building. They were known for their faith. Even in a culture that longed to suppress "the Way" (Acts 9:2), the news spread, and the world was taking note. Vibrant faith stands out.

We might think of a report as something negative because it's so often used to tell someone about inappropriate behavior, but verse 9 is talking about a report that is just a straight telling of the facts. The church in Rome had a vibrant, growing faith that even encouraged the apostle Paul in his faith. So, we have to ask ourselves two questions: Is our faith worth reporting? And if it is, what straight facts would that report tell?

When our faith results in a good report, our friends know it, benefit from it, and are loved because of it.

DELIGHT

What does verse 8 say that Paul did because of the Roman believers' faith? What about in verses 9-10?

Why did Paul want to visit with the believers in Rome?

How has another believer's faith encouraged you? Why is it so important for believers to encourage each other in their faith?

DISPLAY

Paul's love for this body of believers that he didn't know and his desire to encourage them was built on the foundation of their shared faith in Jesus. And all of this was based on a report that made its way from Rome to Corinth. Think about your own life honestly. Then, write a short news blurb or report about your faith in the space provided below. When you finish, ask yourself: What needs to change so that this report points people (especially your friends) to Jesus?

Ask God to help you see what your faith would look like if it were reported to the world. Pray that He would help you see where to grow and which friends and other believers you should connect with to encourage and be encouraged in your faith.

MEMORY VERSE

"NO ONE HAS GREATER LOVE THAN THIS: TO LAY DOWN HIS LIFE FOR HIS FRIENDS."

JOHN 15:13

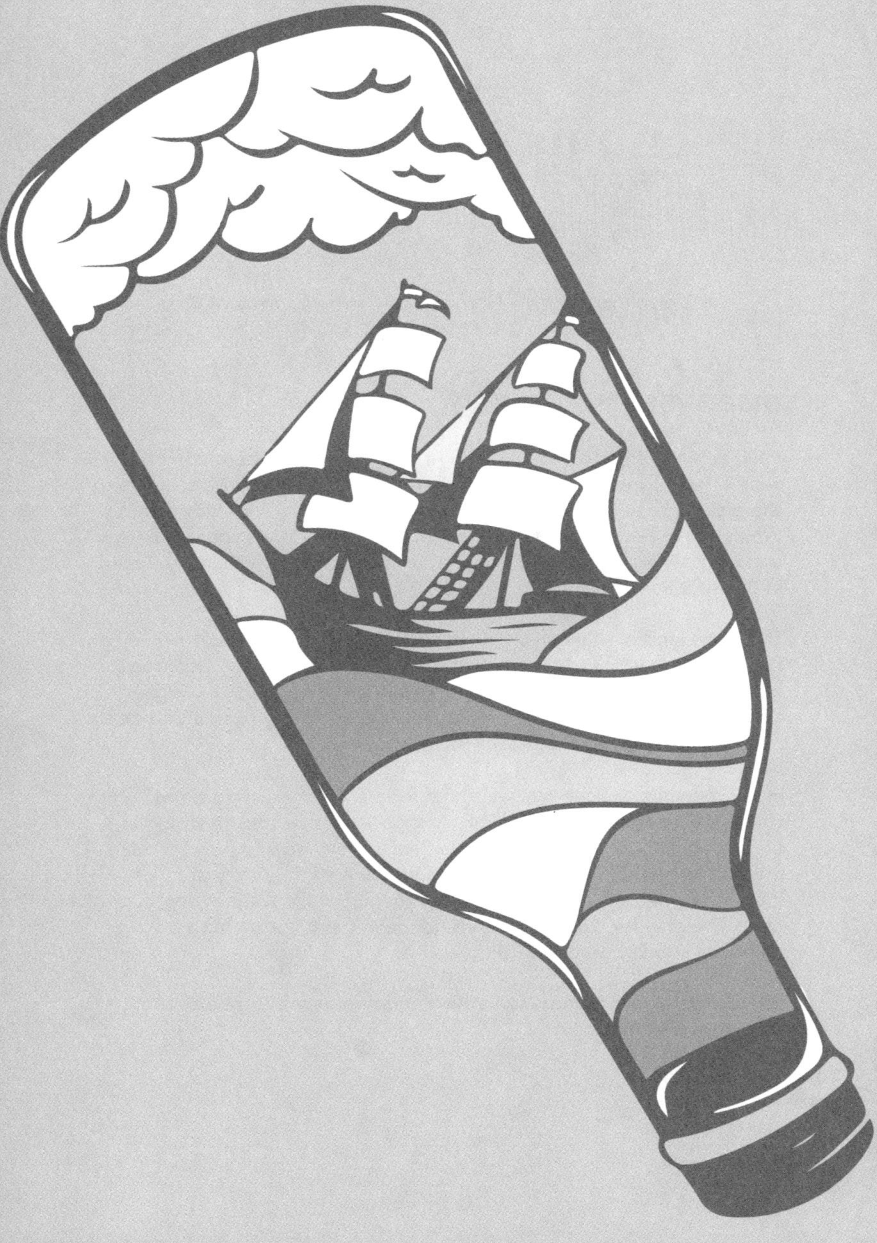

DAY 17

IN ALL TIMES

READ PHILIPPIANS 1:3-11.

I give thanks to my God for every remembrance of you.
— Philippians 1:3

DISCOVER

Imagine you've had a bad day. You're sitting with your back against the wall, knees tugged close to your chest. A friend finds you, sinks down to the ground beside you, and just sits with you until you're ready to talk. When you're ready, your friend listens, then says, "I love you. I'm here, and I'm praying for you." Which of your friends' faces flash in your mind in this situation?

This is the kind of friendship Paul had with the Philippian believers. When Paul wrote his letter to them, neither Paul nor the believers were really in what we'd call a good place. Paul was in prison, and the Philippian church was divided. In these simple facts, we see a key truth about godly relationships: they aren't just for the good times.

In this example, we see two ways that friends are there in all times. In the church we see that we support our friends—whether they're struggling or thriving in God's plan for them. In Paul, we see how to pray for our friends: We thank God for them when we think of them. We pray for them when we miss them. We pray for them joyfully. We pray for them often. We pray for God's work to be done in them, for them to grow in their love and knowledge of Him.

As we pray for our friends, something amazing happens: our love for them grows even more.

DELIGHT

Find Philippians 1:3-11 in your Bible. Highlight or circle any words that point to the ways Paul prayed for the Philippian believers.

What words did Paul use in verses 5 and 7 to describe the relationship he had with the Philippian believers? Would you use this word to describe your friendships? Why or why not?

Why is it important for us to encourage others on their most difficult days?

DISPLAY

Think about the friends whose faces came to mind when you imagined someone being there for you on a tough day. Using Paul's words to the Philippians as a guide, write a short letter to each one of those friends. Tell them why you're thankful for them and how you're praying for them. Then, you have a few options: you can keep the letters and use them to help you pray for those friends, give the letters to your friends now, or hold on to the letters and give them to your friends when they need some extra encouragement during tough times.

Thank God for the friends He has given you who encourage you, support you, and pray for you. Ask God to help you be that kind of friend to them. Pray that you would continue to grow in love of God and one another.

DAY 18

MIND THE LINE

READ JOB 2:11-13.

Then they sat on the ground with him seven days and nights, but no one spoke a word to him because they saw that his suffering was very intense.
— Job 2:13

DISCOVER

Sometimes it feels like bad things come in waves. You'll have only just returned to standing after one wave knocked you down when you see another one cresting on the horizon. Job knew that feeling better than most. Job had been faithful to God. Satan wanted to test Him. God allowed it. And Job lost almost everything.

Job's wife begged him to just "Curse God and die!" (v. 9) But Job refused—he knew God was good, even when bad things came. And that's when his friends showed up.

Eventually, their presence would become a negative thing. But for one week, they showed us exactly what good friends should do: They went to Job specifically to sympathize with and comfort him. They wept and mourned with him. They sat with him in silence. And twice, Scripture says they saw him (see vv. 12-13). We all want to be seen and for someone to notice our pain and sit with us in it. Being a good friend isn't about giving good advice so much as recognizing needs and filling them.

When Job finally spoke, his friends gave speeches riddled with judgment and accusation (see Job 4–5; 8; 11). In Scripture, we can watch them cross the line from helpful to hurtful. And we can learn from them to mind the line when our friends hurt.

DELIGHT

Why is it sometimes easier to respond to our hurting friends the way Job's wife did than the way his friends initially responded?

How have other people been present with you in the same way Job's friends were with him here?

What does it mean to be "seen" when you're hurting? What about for you to "see" someone else who's hurting?

DISPLAY

Even the most joyful person you know struggles at some point—tough times come for us all in various ways. Sometimes our struggles are related to our faith and sometimes they're just part of living in a broken world. But these struggles provide an opportunity for us to be there for our friends, just as God designed us to do. Ask God to help you see friends who are struggling, then write out how you can take each of the following steps to help you "mind the line" with your hurting friends.

Step 1 — See.

Step 2 — Sympathize and Comfort.

Step 3 — Mourn and Weep.

Step 4 — Sit and Be Quiet.

Pray that God would show you how to be a good friend in times of joy and times of sadness. Ask Him to help you see friends who are hurting and how you can sit with them in their pain.

DAY 19

LIKE-SOULED FRIENDS

READ 1 SAMUEL 18:1-3.

*Jonathan made a covenant with David because
he loved him as much as himself.
— 1 Samuel 18:3*

DISCOVER

Jonathan and David were like brothers from another mother; they were tight as tight can be. The friendship they shared formed a bond that was so deep that Jonathan loved David as much as he loved himself. That is a selfless love! This type of bond can occur when two friends are so like-minded that they are like-souled. They connect on a deep level through their common beliefs, interests, and goals.

The CSB says that "Jonathan was bound to David in close friendship" (v. 1), meaning their souls were "bound," "knit," or "tied" together. They were both courageous warriors and men of faith, and God drew them together to support and encourage one another as they followed Him. They were two souls connected by love for God, for one another, and for the people of God.

Even though Jonathan would have normally been the next king, he trusted God's choice in David. Jonathan protected his friend from his own father and vowed that he would always stand by David, his friend and God's chosen king: "You yourself will be king over Israel, and I'll be your second-in-command" (1 Sam. 23:17). Jonathan shows us what it means to love our friends selflessly, recognizing that pursuing God's best is best for everyone—even when it means us giving up something that seems to be rightfully ours.

DELIGHT

How would you describe David and Jonathan's friendship? Does this describe any of your friendships? Explain.

What does Jonathan's humility and love for David show you about the way friendship should be?

What does it show you about the health of your own friendships? What's going well? What needs to change?

DISPLAY

Like-souled friends aren't the people you catch up with every few years or only talk to when you happen to see them. Like-souled friends are the ones who just get you, the ones who you make time for. You might be different, but you have a deep friendship rooted in love of God and each other. These friendships are God-given gifts to help us enjoy life, know love, and follow God well. Who are these friends in your life? Write out their names, then write some specific ways they encourage you and bring joy into your life. Then ask God to show you how to do the same for them. Consider sending a text or writing a note to tell them how thankful you are for them and their friendship.

Thank God for the like-souled friends He has given you. If you don't have a friend you consider like-souled, pray that God would bring a godly friend like that into your life. If you do, pray that God would show you how to love your friends the way Jonathan loved David.

DAY 20

WAIT ON GOD

READ ROMANS 12:9-21.

Friends, do not avenge yourselves; instead, leave room for God's wrath, because it is written, Vengeance belongs to me; I will repay, says the Lord.
— *Romans 12:19*

DISCOVER

God's mercy to us through Jesus allows us to live in ways that please Him. In response to His mercy, believers should want to live all of our lives as an act of worship to God (see Rom. 12:1-2). That includes our friendships, and in these verses, Paul takes away our wondering with plain language. He tells us in simple, active words, exactly how to—and how not to—love our friends.

Then Paul takes things a step further than just telling us how to keep our relationships healthy; he gives instructions for what to do when those relationships fall apart or when people hurt us. Our typical response when people hurt us is to become defensive or reactive but neither response is truly effective.

Thankfully, Paul gives us a better way: respond with compassion and wait on God. This doesn't mean allowing others to hurt us further or not telling the truth. It does mean we refuse to wound others in response. It can be difficult to wait when we're hurting or when someone is telling lies about us and we want others to know the truth. But if we follow God, as we wait on Him to speak for us, our character often speaks to the truth.

DELIGHT

In the space below, make a list of the positive things these verses tell you to do. Then make a list of the negative things the verses tell you to not do. Write a summary sentence about how these actions help you build godly relationships.

Why is it difficult to wait on God to avenge wrongs on our behalf? How does Jesus's victory over sin and death show that waiting on God is always a better way?

DISPLAY

Think of a specific friendship where you're experiencing hurt or someone who's not a friend has hurt you. Look back at the actions you listed. Which of those actions could be helpful in this situation? Write each action that comes to mind in the space provided below, and beside each one, write out how you plan to take this step in that relationship.

Thank God for caring about the hearts of your friends and your heart. Pray that when people hurt you, God will help you to be compassionate and wait on Him.

SECTION 3

DATING

Social media posts, books, and movies in abundance claim to know what love really is and try to make us feel like they can let us in on the secret. But God's Word is the authority over all things—including dating. You might be surprised to find that romance and sex are presented as good and sacred things in God's Word—when we follow God's design for them. So, let's see what Scripture has to say about the way we are called to love our significant others.

DAY 21

WONDER AND WORRY

READ MATTHEW 6:25-34.

But seek first the kingdom of God and his righteousness, and all these things will be provided for you.
— Matthew 6:33

DISCOVER

Whether we want to admit it or not, most of us daydream about the future. Maybe we have specific visions for what careers we'll have, where we'll travel, which of our friends will still be part of our everyday lives, or even who we'll marry. These ideas may seem like distant points on a map, but our hearts already desire to travel there.

Planning for the future is good, but sometimes our wondering causes worry. This entire passage is a message of comfort from Jesus—a promise that the God of the universe knows and will take care of all our needs as we seek His kingdom. Jesus never specifically mentioned if or who you'll marry as one of the worries of the world, but we know it can be.

There's nothing wrong with praying about the "if" and "who" of God's plan for your romantic relationships—God uses marriage as a beautiful picture of the relationship between Him and His people. If you marry, who you'll marry is important, but seeking God is the most important thing. As you seek Him, everything else falls into its rightful place, including our romantic relationships.

DELIGHT

What things does Jesus tell us not to worry about in these verses? Why do you think Jesus would use these as His key points?

Focus on the first few words of verse 28: "Why do you worry?" Spend some time thinking about and praying through your answer.

Jesus assures us that God already knows what we need and provides those things for us as we seek Him. How does this comfort you when it comes to the question of who you'll marry?

DISPLAY

Have you ever thought about who you want to date or wondered about what your spouse would be like if you were to get married? It can be easy to dream about who we'll be or whom we'll be with in the future, but sometimes it's difficult to think about who we are now and the people God is shaping us into. Take a minute to write out a few goals and ideas you have for your future, leaving space below each one. Then, under each item, write out the sentence, "God will shape me into the best _____ as I seek Him." Fill in the blank with roles such as sibling, spouse, designer, athlete, or caretaker.

Ask God to help you follow Him and trust Him with your present, even though you have questions about the future. Pray that you will allow Him to shape you into the person He designed you to be as you follow Him now.

DAY 22

FAMILIAR STORIES

READ GENESIS 2:15-25.

This is why a man leaves his father and mother and bonds with his wife, and they become one flesh. Both the man and his wife were naked, yet felt no shame.
— Genesis 2:24-25

DISCOVER

Think about your favorite stories—movies you've watched again and again, books good enough to reread, or shows you've binged on repeat. The details of these stories often become so familiar to us that they slip into the background. Depending on how long you've been a Christian or part of a church, some Bible stories can start to feel that way too. But although Scripture doesn't change, it is always relevant and working in our lives (see John 17:17; 2 Tim. 3:16-17; Heb. 4:12).

So, even when the stories become familiar, they still matter. God created humanity with a specific design: to have emotions, intellect, will, and the capacity for relationships. Despite what culture says, God uniquely and purposefully designed men and women to accomplish His plan for the world. Even though we often want to think we know best, God's design and plan are perfect—they need no tweaks from us. And part of God's plan for humanity includes marriage between one man and one woman for life.

Though Scripture doesn't talk about dating, dating isn't meaningless. The people you date are also created in the image of God, and you need to treat them with respect and care. Whom you choose to date matters, too. The right person will lead you closer to God, but the wrong one will lead you further away.

DELIGHT

Have you ever allowed Scripture to become so familiar that the stories seemed not to matter as much? How can you guard yourself against this happening in the future?

Why is it important for us to know and follow God's design for dating and marriage?

What is the most difficult part of living out God's design for dating and marriage in a culture that often calls His way intolerant or ignorant?

DISPLAY

Though we seek to embrace and live out God's design for the world and our lives, we recognize that sin has distorted that plan. Dating in God's way might be a struggle for you, but that doesn't mean it's impossible. Struggle doesn't have to lead to sin. You might struggle with a desire to engage in sexual activity, the temptation to view pornography, same-sex attraction, or staying faithful to the person you're dating. These desires and struggles are part of living in a broken world, but giving into them doesn't have to be part of your story. Think about the following ways you can set yourself up to not fall into sin in your dating relationships.

1. **Make time to study God's Word and pray.**

2. **Surround yourself with friends you can be open and honest with. Share your struggles.**

3. **Be involved in your student ministry and/or Christian groups at school.**

4. **Find a more mature believer who can mentor you in your faith.**

5. **If you have trauma related to these struggles, seek a counselor who can help you process and heal.**

Praise God for designing men and women differently and with specific purposes. Pray that God would help you live out His design for your life when it comes to your dating relationships. Ask God to give you the wisdom to seek help when you struggle.

DAY 23

THE MISSING INGREDIENT

READ 1 CORINTHIANS 13:1-3.

If I speak human or angelic tongues but do not have love, I am a noisy gong or a clanging cymbal.
— 1 Corinthians 13:1

DISCOVER

Have you ever tried to cook something and left out just one ingredient or accidentally added salt instead of sugar? A missing or wrong ingredient can change the entire taste, texture, or flavor of a dish. Without all of the ingredients functioning as they should, the dish simply fails.

Similarly, Paul said that if we claim to follow Jesus but don't have love, we will fail. We can do all kinds of good things in the name of God, but without love propelling that good, our actions are meaningless. While Paul spoke in these verses about love in general terms, these principles can easily be applied to our dating relationships.

When we date, how we treat our boyfriend or girlfriend matters, and just like anything else in life, how we treat people goes deeper than our actions. Just like you can tell if an ingredient is missing in a recipe, you can tell when the heart behind someone's actions is off. When we say we love someone, this is verified by our actions. If we mistreat someone or encourage them to go beyond their boundaries or comfort level, we are not showing them love. Love, as we'll see throughout 1 Corinthians 13, is selfless.

Ultimately, dating—or any relationship—boils down to love. If we don't show real, selfless love and seek the best for the other person in our relationships, we are basically just using that person for our selfish desires.

DELIGHT

Why is the guiding force of our actions so important? Why is love such a vital guiding force?

When has selfless love been a missing ingredient in one of your relationships? How can you make sure selfless love is a part of all of your relationships moving forward?

Have you ever been in a relationship where the person said he or she was for you, but the person didn't seem to be motivated by love or a desire for your good? What was that like?

DISPLAY

Paul mentioned three actions that are meaningless without love: our words, our knowledge and faith, and our gifts. Use the following questions to think through the way you treat your closest friends or the people you date.

Do I speak kindly to my friends and/or the people I date? Why or why not?

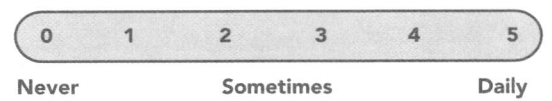

| 0 | 1 | 2 | 3 | 4 | 5 |

Never   **Sometimes**   **Daily**

How well do I know my friends and/or the people I date beyond the simple facts about their lives?

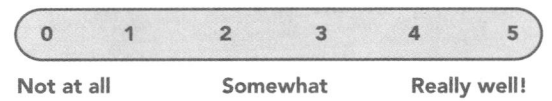

| 0 | 1 | 2 | 3 | 4 | 5 |

Not at all   **Somewhat**   **Really well!**

What needs to change in your life to speak more kindly and to go beyond the surface in your relationships?

Ask God to grow your love for Him first, and through that, grow your love for others. Pray that He will give you a pure and respectful love for the people you date and show you how to act toward them out of that love.

DAY 24

THE DATING QUESTION

READ 1 CORINTHIANS 13:4-7.

*Love is patient, love is kind. Love does not envy,
is not boastful, is not arrogant . . .*
— *1 Corinthians 13:4*

DISCOVER

Paul said that anything done without love is just noise. Without love, relationships fail. Love is about the motives in our hearts, which are displayed in our words and actions (see Luke 6:45). When love is in our hearts, it spills out in our actions. Here's what that should look like in our dating relationships.

We are patient and kind toward those we date, considering their needs above our own. We rejoice when they succeed. We are compassionate when they hurt, and we humbly apologize when we're the creators of that hurt. We encourage them to keep seeking God and the good of others. We are friends first. We are gentle when we're hurt and quick to forgive. We endure on the tough days as God endures with us.

Romance might seem dreamy and fun and exciting—and in the right context, it can be. But before we get tangled up in romantic ideals, we have to realize that, at its core, dating is about asking a key question: "Do we serve God better together or apart?"

This means that before you ever pursue a person with dating in mind, you should seek God. He has given you the Holy Spirit to act as your personal guide in how to live life His way—and that includes dating. These dos and do nots go a long way in forming a foundation of respect and love that will carry you through all kinds of relationships—including dating and marriage.

DELIGHT

Which of these qualities of love is most difficult for you to live out? Which is the easiest? Why?

What would it look like for you to seek God above seeking a romantic relationship or the person you're dating? How do you think that would change your relationships moving forward?

DISPLAY

Our actions never happen in a vacuum; they always affect someone else. What you do in your dating relationships now will have a lasting effect on your heart—and on the hearts of the people you date. This effect ripples into their families now and into future relationships. We must remember no one belongs to us. We might call the people we date "our" boyfriend or girlfriend, but they ultimately and only belong to God. The relationships He gifts to us are to be treasured and cultivated, not trashed and crushed.

If you're dating, write out your boyfriend or girlfriend's name in the space below. Then write out each of the qualities of love Paul listed and rank how you're doing in your relationship on a scale of 1 to 10. Look at your weak areas and write out ideas of ways you can love better in those areas.

If you're not dating, list the qualities of love and write out ideas for how you can do each of those in dating relationships in the future.

> If you're dating someone, ask God to show you where you aren't loving that person well and ask Him to help you to change. Then ask Him to show you where you are doing well and how you can continue to grow in loving well. If you aren't dating, pray that God would grow your love for Him and all other people around you.

DAY 25

HOW NOT TO LOVE

READ 1 CORINTHIANS 13:4-7 AGAIN.

Love . . . is not rude, is not self-seeking, is not irritable, and does not keep a record of wrongs.
— 1 Corinthians 13:4-5

DISCOVER

Yesterday's devotion focused on how to love well, but today is more about seeing how not to love well. Whether phrased in negative or positive language, we can look at each of the traits of love that Paul mentioned in these verses and see a clear instruction of how not to show love. We do not show love by being impatient, mean, arrogant, rude, selfish, irritable, suspicious, or pessimistic. We do not show love by bragging, lying, rejoicing in wrong actions or others' mistakes, or giving up when things get tough.

God's love for us is good and beautiful, and He designed love in our relationships with others to be the same way. But sometimes we struggle and fall. When we do, we must turn to God, ask for forgiveness, and lean into the Holy Spirit for help in getting back on the right track.

However, there's also a key truth in Scripture we often overlook when we're really interested in someone: dating someone who does not share our beliefs about God is never a good idea (see 2 Cor. 6:14). While it's entirely possible for someone who knows God to still be working on changing these traits as she or he grows closer to God or for that person to be struggling in his or her faith, it's important to ask: Is this the pattern of that person's life? If it is, then that's not a relationship you need to pursue.

DELIGHT

Which of these negative traits is most difficult to see in yourself? In others? Explain.

Why is it not a good idea to date someone who doesn't share your faith in Jesus?

Are there any relationships you need to let go of or decide not to pursue? Why or why not?

DISPLAY

Use the columns provided to see which of these negative traits show up consistently in your life or in the life of the person you're dating. You could also fill it in for your best friend—those relationships are vital too!

TRAIT	ME	GIRL/BOYFRIEND OR BEST FRIEND
Impatient	○	○
Mean	○	○
Arrogant	○	○
Rude	○	○
Selfish	○	○
Irritable	○	○
Suspicious	○	○
Pessimistic	○	○
Bragging	○	○
Lying	○	○
Rejoicing in Wrongs	○	○
Giving Up	○	○

Are you the kind of person you want to date? If not, ask God to help you be more like Jesus.

Pray that God would help you see yourself accurately—how you've grown and how you still need to grow. Ask Him to help you see when a dating relationship is okay to start, ones that should never start, and ones that might need to end. Invite God to be the center of all of your relationships.

DAY 26

SUPPRESSED TRUTH

READ 1 CORINTHIANS 13:4-7 AGAIN.

Love finds no joy in unrighteousness but rejoices in the truth.
— 1 Corinthians 13:6

DISCOVER

Have you ever struggled to admit the truth to yourself because you just didn't want to be wrong—or right—about something? For instance, maybe there was a time when you felt a cold coming on, but you didn't want to admit that you felt crummy because it would keep you from doing things you were looking forward to.

Sometimes it's tough to admit the truth when we've known it deep down all along, and that includes spiritual truths. Scripture says all people have the capacity to recognize the truth about God (see Rom. 1:19), but they "suppress the truth" (Rom. 1:18) in their own hearts through sin and for others by not sharing it.

Not knowing the truth before we date is dangerous. God has a specific design for dating, marriage, and sex. But society says God's design is flawed—that all people have the freedom to do whatever we want, whenever we want, with whomever we want as long as it's consensual and we're in love. Society even encourages many of the actions Paul said belonged to the unrighteous—those who live in opposition to God and His Word (see 1 Cor. 6:9-11).

But God's Word is truth (see John 17:17), and by it we can determine what is true and what is not. God's Word says love "finds no joy in unrighteousness" (1 Cor. 13:6). The righteous have a right relationship with God through Jesus, and their actions reflect that. They show God gratitude for all He has done and glorify Him with their words, their bodies, and their lives (see Rom. 12:1; 1 Cor. 6:20; Eph. 4:29). This means they honor His design for love and romance, even if it isn't popular.

DELIGHT

When did you know something was right or true but chose to do or believe the opposite? Why?

Why is it difficult to stay true to God's design for dating, sex, and marriage? Even though it's hard, why is it best?

DISPLAY

People who try to convince you to do something you know to be wrong do not have your best interests at heart. You might want to believe they do, but deep down, you know love isn't selfish—it seeks what's best for the other person (see v. 5). The more we suppress what we know to be right, the easier it is to be convinced to do what we know is wrong. In the space below, create a plan to stay focused on God when it's tough. Consider who can walk with you and encourage you, what Scripture will help, and what other support you need (such as family, friends, books, or Bible studies).

Who can walk with you and encourage you?

What Scripture can help you?

What other support do you need?

> **Thank God for pursuing you and helping you know truth. Pray that He will help you see the truth and make difficult decisions. Ask Him to help you stay strong when someone else tries to convince you to do something wrong.**

Love is patient, love is kind. Love does not envy, is not boastful, is not arrogant, is not rude, is not self-seeking, is not irritable, and does not keep a record of wrongs.

MEMORY VERSE

1 CORINTHIANS 13:4-7

Love finds no joy in unrighteousness but rejoices in the truth. It bears all things, believes all things, hopes all things, endures all things.

DAY 27

LEVELS

READ 1 CORINTHIANS 13:4-7 AGAIN.

*Love . . . bears all things, believes all things,
hopes all things, endures all things.*
— *1 Corinthians 13:4,7*

DISCOVER

Consider any kind of game you play that has different levels or stages. Typically, you have to retrieve certain objects or cards before you progress to the next round. It can be frustrating to stay on the same level while you work toward the next. You see others happily and effortlessly moving forward, but sometimes it takes you several attempts before you can move forward. Every level has some similarities, yet each one brings new challenges, new successes, and new excitement.

Love has levels, too. Love when you're dating isn't the same as love when you're married. Dating is like round one, where you're trying to figure out if the person you're interested in or dating is someone you could spend your life with. Dating is more restricted, helping us get to know one another with guarded hearts and bodies. Dating is not designed for exploring sexually but for exploring the possibility that this person could be a future spouse.

Marriage is like the final level, where the decisions have been made and two people have grown closer, determining that they work well together. Dating helps deepen relationships in perseverance, trust, hope, and in enduring tough things, gradually moving closer to the marriage level. However, the level of intimacy in dating is not the same as it is in marriage. It's only in marriage that the two make lifelong vows and become one (see Mark 10:8).

DELIGHT

Why is it important to know the way someone you date handles conflict and pursues personal and spiritual growth?

Since the purpose of dating is to help us explore whether or not someone would make a good spouse for us in the future, what are some "red flags" (spiritual, emotional, or physical) that we should watch out for in our dating relationships?

How does dating being more restricted protect us?

DISPLAY

Here's the truth: human beings were made to desire intimacy. God created sexual intimacy to be good and God-honoring, but only in the right context: within a marriage relationship. But hear this: if you sin sexually, you are not doomed. You are not beyond redemption. You are not beyond God's reach or His compassion. He loves you still and He always will. But any sin requires us to repent—to let it go and turn to God for forgiveness and restoration. The truth is, whether in our thoughts, with our eyes, or with our bodies, all of us struggle with sexual temptation and sin to some degree. Take a minute to sit quietly and identify your struggle. Read the prayer prompt below, then write out the names of one or two "safe" people—godly people you can trust—and consider sharing your struggle with them.

Imagine yourself holding that struggle in your hands and setting it at God's feet. Pour out your heart to Him, asking for forgiveness and restoration where necessary and strength and wisdom to follow His design for dating and marriage.

DAY 28

THE FULL PICTURE

READ 1 CORINTHIANS 13:8-12.

When I was a child, I spoke like a child, I thought like a child, I reasoned like a child. When I became a man, I put aside childish things.
— 1 Corinthians 13:11

DISCOVER

Have you ever done a scavenger hunt? You get one clue at a time to guide you to the next one. You know something good waits at the end, but you're not exactly sure where that might be. You've been given some details, but you won't have the whole story until you reach the end.

Life is a little like that too. Like clues in a scavenger hunt, there are things we need to help us grow with God. Spiritual gifts are among those things, and the Corinthians were arguing over which ones were best (see 1 Cor. 12:4-11). But Paul basically said, "Hey, those things are good, but they aren't eternal. They're not for you to use selfishly but to help you know God. When you see Him face to face, those things won't matter anymore. But love will always matter."

Sometimes we pursue the wrong things in our dating relationships too. It's easy to think that right now is the best it will ever be and justify doing something that isn't God-honoring because we don't see the full picture. Dating takes the humility to acknowledge that we don't exactly know what God has planned for our future—or the future of the person we're dating. It takes wisdom to acknowledge that as limited people, we need boundaries to help us stay on the right track. Above all, successful dating takes an unselfish "God first" and "others first" kind of perspective and love.

DELIGHT

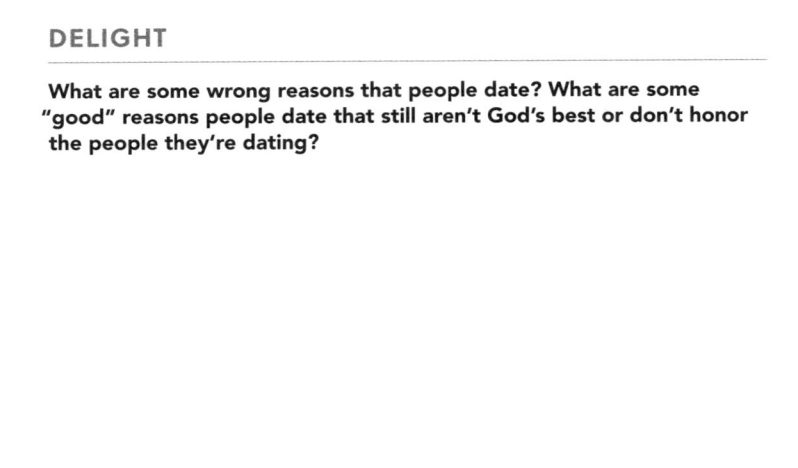

What are some wrong reasons that people date? What are some "good" reasons people date that still aren't God's best or don't honor the people they're dating?

How does seeing that you don't know the full picture help you understand the need for boundaries and wisdom in dating?

DISPLAY

Look at the three characteristics we highlighted that are necessary in dating: humility, wisdom, and love. Then think about the kinds of things you do or could pursue in dating relationships that don't fall in those categories. The truth is, dating isn't just about us—first it's about glorifying God, and then it's about pursuing the good of the person you date. Take a minute to think about which of the three areas you most need to grow in if you're dating or if you want to date someone. If you get stuck, ask yourself: How can I honor God and the person I'm dating by pursuing _____?

Thank God for showing us what love is and how to love well. Ask God to fill you with love for all the people around you and to help you be wise about how you love others, especially when you choose to date someone.

DAY 29

A CASUAL ACCEPTANCE

READ 1 CORINTHIANS 13:13.

*Now these three remain: faith, hope, and love —
but the greatest of these is love.
— 1 Corinthians 13:13*

DISCOVER

Love doesn't end. Life is "like a vapor" (James 4:14), and very few of the things that matter to us here on earth will matter in eternity. But love will, and strangely enough, faith and hope will, too.

Faith means trusting in something we can't see or that we have not seen come true yet. Hope is the anticipation we hold onto until what we're waiting for happens. At some point, both of these will fade because what we've had faith in and hope for will come true in Jesus. This is why Paul said that love is the greatest of the three.

In the world's eyes, love is mostly about emotion or attraction. However, the love Paul described in 1 Corinthians 13 runs deeper—it starts in our hearts. Today we tend to think of the "heart" in terms of emotions, but in the Bible, the word for "heart" refers to the center of our mind, will, and emotions—the place within us where our thoughts, feelings, speech, and actions come from (see Luke 6:45).[8] This is why Scripture says it's so important for us to "guard," or protect, our hearts (see Prov. 4:23).

So much of our world treats our hearts, minds, and bodies casually, saying we can do whatever we want with them without consequence. But the way we live now and treat our hearts—and others' hearts—matters. Even though we know Jesus will bring healing when He returns (see Rev. 21:5), we should regard hearts—our own and others'—with eternity in mind.

8. Gerald P. Cowen, "Heart," in *Holman Illustrated Bible Dictionary*, ed. Chad Brand et al. (Nashville, TN: Holman Bible Publishers, 2003), 731, Logos Bible Software edition.

DELIGHT

What do you sometimes think is greater than love? What do you need in order to make this kind of love a priority in your life?

How can you "guard your heart" in a world that often treats it casually?

How have you treated someone else's heart casually? What do you need to do to make it right?

DISPLAY

Unlike the world, Scripture never says to treat our hearts, minds, or bodies casually. Instead, we're called to be careful, loving, and compassionate with all that we are and treat others the same way. In what areas of your life are you too casual, flippant, or indifferent about your heart, your mind, and your body? Below each area, write some ideas for how you can be more intentional in honoring your heart, mind, and body the way God intended.

HEART	MIND	BODY

Ask God to help you see how to care for your heart, mind, and body the way God intended. Seek forgiveness for times when you haven't treated others with that same care. Pray that you would always seek to love and care for the hearts of others.

DAY 30

APPRECIATION AND ANTICIPATION

READ SONG OF SONGS 2:1-17.

Young women of Jerusalem, I charge you by the gazelles and the wild does of the field, do not stir up or awaken love until the appropriate time.
— Song of Songs 2:7

DISCOVER

It might surprise you to know that God's Word talks openly about sex. In Song of Songs, a man known for his wisdom had some wisdom to share about dating and sexual desire. God designed us for intimacy with Him and others, but sexual intimacy is a special gift meant to be enjoyed within the sacredness and safety of marriage. God's plan for us is good—it's not to take away our joy and pleasure but to make our joy and our lives full (see John 10:10).

Before the man's wedding, the passion and desire were there between him and his bride to be, but so was the restraint. To him, she was a standout, a beauty, and he was proud to be seen with her (see vv. 2,4,10); her voice was sweet and her face lovely (see v. 14). To her, he was a safe place; he cared for her (see v. 5). He was attractive, strong, and athletic (see vv. 3,8-9), and he "looked on [her] with love" (v. 4). Yet, we see that they did not pursue sexual activity together until their wedding night (see 4:12).

So, the man's bride gave a wise warning to other young people, including us: "Do not stir up or awaken love until the appropriate time" (v. 7).

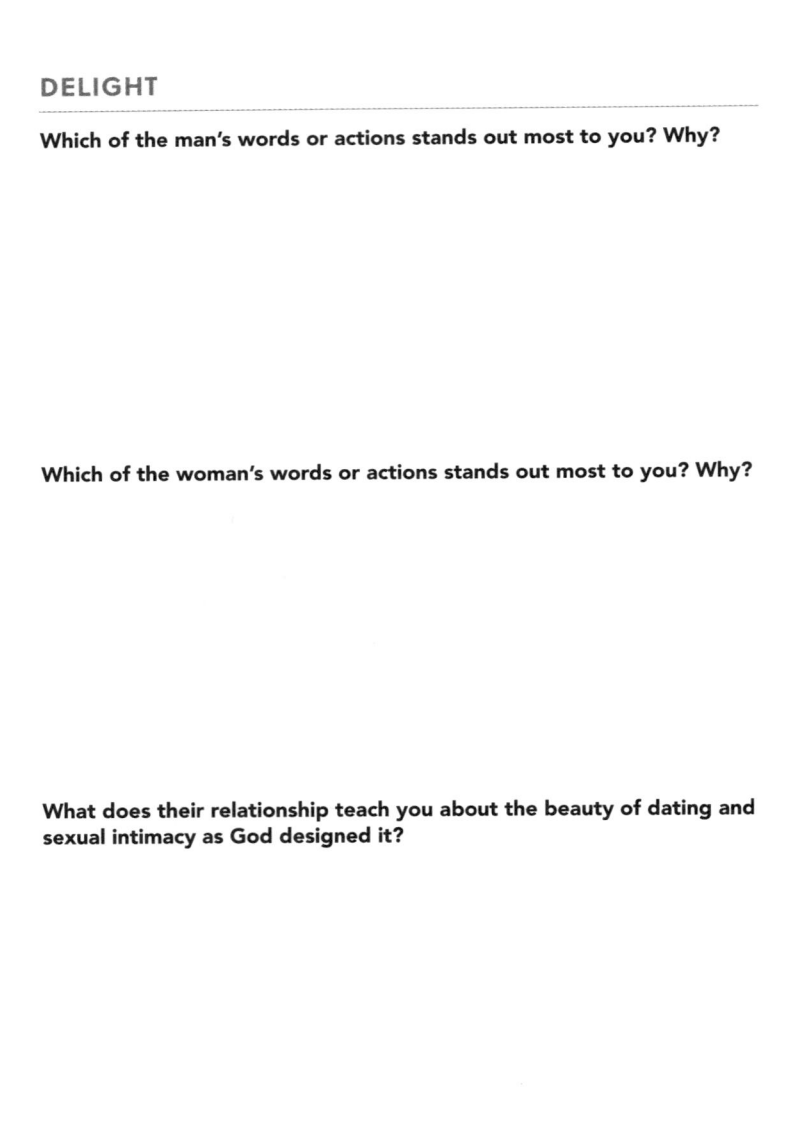

DELIGHT

Which of the man's words or actions stands out most to you? Why?

Which of the woman's words or actions stands out most to you? Why?

What does their relationship teach you about the beauty of dating and sexual intimacy as God designed it?

DISPLAY

Seeing the way the man and his future bride spoke to each other confirms something we already know: our desires don't disappear just because we know we should wait. God created us with soul-deep passion and a need for love, but He also created us to seek Him and use wisdom. It's important to respectfully appreciate the people God puts in our lives through dating For instance, focusing too much on physical appearance and spending time alone together with a person we're dating can push us toward a dangerous line. Use the words and actions in these verses to journal about how you should treat anyone you date, either now or in the future.

Thank God for giving you wisdom through His Word and His Spirit. Pray that you would use that wisdom in your dating relationships and learn to view sexual intimacy according to God's good design.

TOXIC TRAITS

You've probably heard someone call a person, group, environment, or behavior "toxic." The word "toxic" describes something poisonous, even to the point of causing death. This definition can apply to relationships, too: certain behaviors and experiences might bring a kind of death to those relationships or can be unhealthy or even unsafe influences in our lives.

We need to be careful about assigning labels to people, but we can certainly recognize—and call out, when appropriate—relationships and behaviors that are harmful. Toxic behaviors might not be exactly what you think, either. They can include physical, mental, and emotional abuse, but it can be tough to pinpoint exactly which specific harmful behaviors can be called "toxic."

If you're wondering whether a relationship is toxic (even within your family), compare it to the following list.

1. The person threatens violence, acts aggressively, or commits physical harm against you or someone else.

2. The person uses words, tones, or volume to communicate that you or someone else is "less than." This can include sarcasm or even picking on someone "good naturedly" when it's clear the recipient feels embarrassed or hurt.

3. You feel anxious or depressed when you are around the person or even when you consider being around him or her.

4. The person is excessively critical, constantly says you're to blame, tries to manipulate you with emotions, guilt, promises, or throws past mistakes in your face. Or the person tries to control you, telling you what you can think, feel, believe, say, or do or who you can talk to or befriend. She or he may also try to limit where you're allowed to go in a way that goes above and beyond a normal concern for safety.

5. The person dismisses your needs or treats you like your personality and preferences do not matter. This could include manipulating you, forcing you to do things you don't want to do that are not necessary or good for you, or telling you he or she wishes you would be like someone else.

6. The person gives excessive punishment when you break rules, or the rules that he or she sets are constantly changing. This type of punishment exceeds the kind of healthy discipline from parents or guardians that is designed to help you grow.

7. The person puts her or his needs before yours the majority of the time.

8. The person gives you the silent treatment instead of explaining a punishment or talking it out.

9. The person believes he or she is always in the right; he or she is the victim every time there is conflict.

10. The person texts and calls excessively and is easily angered or accuses you of not caring if you don't answer right away. Again, this is beyond healthy supervision and care and concern from parents or guardians.

11. The person doesn't like it when you spend time with other people.

12. Your relationship isn't give-and-take—you do most of the giving; the other person does most of the taking.

13. The person constantly wants you to lie for her or him, or you feel the need to lie about your relationship with her or him.

14. You feel like you have to hide certain parts of yourself when you're around the person in order to be okay.

15. Rather than feeling uplifted after being in the person's presence, you feel empty and exhausted.

16. The person often declares that what you want to do is "stupid," and/or you always end up doing what he or she wants to do.

These sixteen items help you identify toxic traits in others. However, it's important and necessary to try to identify toxic traits in yourself as well. Would your friends or family check yes for any of these items when thinking of you?

The truth is, we all have the tendency to be "toxic" or engage in toxic behaviors because we are all born with a sin-nature that screams at us to live for and look out for ourselves. But followers of Jesus don't stay there—we have been redeemed from our toxicity too. We can walk in a new life, paving the way to peace for and with all the people around us.

TOXIC LOVE

What can we do if we find ourselves in a toxic relationship or family situation?

First, we should seek God above all else. This is the path to peace in our own lives that flows into the lives of others. You can even use this devotional as a tool to help point you in the right direction.

Next, consider the following steps and ideas.

Pray It Out — Before you approach a person who consistently harms you in some way, pray about it. Seek God's wisdom about how to and even if it's safe to confront this person. Pray for him or her to find healing and wholeness in God. What relationships do you need to pray about right now?

Seek Out — Talk to someone you know you can trust who will pray with you and share godly wisdom with you. Who in your family could be a safe place for you to seek wisdom? Who among your church family and friends could be a safe place for you to seek wisdom?

Talk It Out — If, after praying and seeking wise counsel, you do believe you should approach the other person, make sure to season your speech with grace (see Col. 4:6) and speak the truth in love (see Eph. 4:15). Decide ahead of time what you want to say. Write it out if that feels best to you. You can even tell the other person that you want to read the letter to her or him. Whatever you do, don't dish out blame. Instead, try using "I feel" or "Here's what I'm telling myself about . . ." when you approach the issue. Depending on the situation, it could be a good idea to meet in a public place or take a safe person with you, even if that person sits a table away.

Grab a journal or sheet of paper and try writing a letter to someone who hurt you. Be honest, use "I" language, and speak the truth in love. Tip: It can—again, depending on the situation—be a good idea to own up to your own mistakes or issues in the relationship.

Speak Out — If someone is abusing you in any way and you do not feel safe, seek help. If it's family, find another safe adult to talk to—maybe a pastor, small group leader, friend's parent, teacher, coach, or someone else in your daily life. Be open and honest. Depending on the situation, you may also consider reaching out to a counselor, medical professional, or law enforcement professional.

Get Out — Sometimes, you need to remove yourself from the situation. With familial abuse, this is a little more complicated. This is why it's important to have other trusted adults you can reach out to. In friendships or dating relationships, though, you do have an immediate option—call it off and get out. This doesn't mean you don't talk to God and work to forgive that person; it just means you do that from a distance. That person does not need to have access to your body, your mind, or your heart anymore.

If you have experienced abuse of any kind through a toxic relationship or someone's toxic behaviors, know that this is not God's design and it breaks His heart. God's commands for you to love and honor others don't mean doing things—or "putting up with" things—that are harmful to you or others. Loving people well sometimes might mean calling out their harmful behaviors to them or finding someone else who can help if it's not safe to talk directly with those people. So do what you need to do: seek God, seek wise counsel, speak out, and get out if it comes to that. Above all, know that you are deeply loved by a God who wants you to have safety, security, and joy all the days of your life.

Sources

Arzt, Nicole. "Toxic Friends: 13 Signs of a Toxic Friendship." Choosing Therapy, September 8, 2023. https://www.choosingtherapy.com/toxic-friends/.

Cleveland Clinic. "How to Tell if You Have a Toxic Parent." October 19, 2021, https://health.clevelandclinic.org/toxic-parenting-traits/.

Greenberg, Jennifer. "Honoring Your Father When He's Evil." The Gospel Coalition, June 18, 2021. https://www.thegospelcoalition.org/article/honoring-father-evil/.

Kolber, Aundi. *Strong Like Water*. Carol Stream, IL: Tyndale Refresh, 2023.

Kolber, Aundi. *Try Softer*. Carol Stream, IL: Tyndale Refresh, 2020.

McDonald, Sabrina Beasley. "How Can You Honor Parents When You Feel They Don't Deserve It?" Family Life. https://www.familylife.com/articles/topics/life-issues/relationships/honoring-your-parents/how-can-you-honor-parents-when-you-feel-they-dont-deserve-it/.

Pemberton, Taryn. "When Friendship Turns Sour: Signs of a Toxic Friend." Spokane Christian Counseling, September 2, 2022. https://spokanechristiancounseling.com/articles/when-friendship-turns-sour-signs-of-a-toxic-friend.

Regan, Sarah. "9 Signs of a Toxic Family & How to Deal with It, from Therapists." MBGHealth, March 17, 2023. https://www.mindbodygreen.com/articles/toxic-families.

LIFEWAY STUDENT DEVOTIONS
Engage with God's Word.

lifeway.com/teendevotionals

- TAKE UP AND FOLLOW 
- THE SHEPHERD KING 
- CHARACTER & COURAGE 
- WORDS OF WISDOM 
- PIONEER & PERFECTOR 
- WITH YOU 
- ROMANS 
- LOVE AND JUSTICE 
- CALLED TO THIS 
- GROWING IN GRATITUDE 
- GOD WITH US 
- MADE NEW